DESIRE LINES

A YEAR OF CELTIC SAINTS

CATHERINE MOONEY

with photographs by **THOMAS JOSHUA COOPER**

DESIRE LINES

A YEAR OF CELTIC SAINTS

CATHERINE MOONEY

with photographs by **THOMAS JOSHUA COOPER**

NATIONAL GALLERIES OF SCOTLAND
EDINBURGH

CONTENTS

7   Director's Foreword

9   In Conversation:
       Thomas Joshua Cooper,
       Catherine Mooney
       and Anne Lyden

17   Desire Lines: A Year of Celtic Saints

106   Biographies of the Saints

112   Acknowledgements

DIRECTOR'S FOREWORD

There are more than six hundred Celtic saints known to us today, and likely more existed. These men and women practised faith and kindness between the fourth and eighth centuries. Travelling across Scotland, Ireland, Wales and Northern England, their journeys and lives are, for the most part, long forgotten, but their legacies can be found today through place names in our villages, towns and surrounding countryside.

Partners Catherine (Kate) Mooney and Thomas Joshua Cooper set out to explore these saintly peregrinations, embarking on their own spiritual and physical journey as they visited the associated sites to create a compendium of photographs. During the Covid pandemic in 2020, when lockdowns curtailed movement and limited international travel, they found themselves embarking on a pastime of tracking down the local saints one by one, without realising it would grow into a very moving and distinct body of work, replete with a sense of home and the passing of time. Thomas, a renowned photographer with a career spanning six decades, has previously travelled all over the world, often for months at a time, with his 1898 view camera in tow. Kate, a silversmith, has endured these long absences from their home in Glasgow. The Saints project was the first creative project they worked on together.

The book is based on a calendar of saints – a long-standing tradition of organising the Christian church year by liturgical seasons and arranging the saints according to their feast days (which are something of a moveable feast, with many conflicting sources on facts obscured over time). Readers are invited to peruse the book at their leisure, to perhaps have it open at a certain date to allow for reflection and reverie. From the view on Loch Lomond representing the feast day of St Kentigerna on 7 January to the scene from Easter Ross representing the feast day of St Fittick on 23 December, the reader is invited to move throughout the calendar year, with views from all over Scotland and its surrounding nations.

The reach and influence of the Celtic saints extend far and wide, and it is somewhat fitting that we offer thanks to our benefactors in North America who made this book possible through the generous support of the American Patrons of the National Library and Galleries of Scotland, alongside that of the Patrons of the National Galleries of Scotland. I had the privilege of shepherding this book over the years in my former role of Chief Curator of Photography, and also conducted the interview with Kate and Thomas that features within these pages. Our Publishing team – Ann Crawford, Catherine Aitken and Jonny Clowes – were instrumental in steering and shaping the beautiful book that is before you. Lastly, immense gratitude is due to Kate and Thomas, without whom we would not have these saintly pictures. The seventy-nine black-and-white photographs that comprise this book also form a generous gift of artworks to the National Galleries of Scotland. I would like to extend my thanks to them both for this wonderful donation, which is a most welcome addition to the permanent collection and will ensure that the legacy of the saints continues for future generations.

Anne Lyden
Director General
National Galleries of Scotland

IN CONVERSATION:
**THOMAS JOSHUA COOPER,
CATHERINE MOONEY**
AND **ANNE LYDEN**

25 May 2023

ANNE LYDEN
We're gathered today on what is the feast day of St Dúnchad, who ruled the abbey at Iona in Scotland. He is one of more than sixty saints from late antiquity – the fourth to eighth centuries – that feature in this book. Can you describe this project and how it came to be?

CATHERINE MOONEY
The project was initially a curiosity about how St Mungo travelled from Culross, Fife to Glasgow, Strathclyde. In 2011 Thomas was invited by Joe Logan, who founded the St Mungo Festival in Glasgow, to judge an art competition. As a thank you Thomas was given an icon of St Mungo – the patron saint of the city. Joe then invited us to the inaugural Molendinar Lecture in 2012 as part of the St Mungo Festival. Listening to Mario Conti, then Archbishop of Glasgow, talk about the history of Glasgow, my mind wandered at a tangent to where was St Mungo from, how did he get here? He seemed to be associated with the Molendinar Burn; I visited a few sites on the Molendinar – Hogganfield Loch and Stepps. It was really quite pretty. I went home and told Thomas what I'd been doing and then he said, could he come with me? And when I took him back, his first response was, we have to go and get my camera. We decided to re-enact the route from Culross (Mungo's birthplace) to Glasgow, following as closely as possible the Antonine Wall ancillary roads.

Initially we worked close to home, working at places associated with St Mungo, including his mother, St Enoch, his mentor, St Serf of Culross, and local people like St Mirren who is associated with the town of Paisley, and the first patron saint of Scotland St Kessog, who lived by Loch Lomond, and St Columba who famously met St Mungo at Kilmacolm, Inverclyde.

AL
Thomas, your interest in saints predates this project, can you tell us about the early saints pictures?

THOMAS JOSHUA COOPER
The first saints pictures that I made, were made for two different reasons. The first one is because I became besotted by St Brendan the Navigator. I made a picture in 2002 at the sea point of his birthplace in Ireland, and he became in many ways, literally and figuratively, the patron of the kind

of wandering that I went through to make the Atlas of Emptiness and Extremity that resulted in *The World's Edge* (2019).

And I was thrilled by his public apology called *Navigatio*, suggesting that out of penance or curiosity or curiosity and penance he may have been one of the first people to have sailed across the Atlantic. I was incredibly inspired by this and worked with his journeys from Ireland to the west coast of Africa, and from the west coast of Africa to Lanzarote, in the Canaries. And there found, amongst other things, that Brendan was one of three patron saints of the Canary Islands, and it is presumed somewhere along the line he began a series of oceanic pilgrimages or journeys of contemplation that could have led him across the ocean to a point that he describes in *Navigatio* as Ultima Thule.

At the same time, in 2002, I was given an opportunity by Sophie Crichton Stuart to do some work on the island of Bute. And what I found in relation to that is that Brendan is the patron saint of Bute, and native-born Bute people are called Brandanes.

CM
Thomas had been to Bute before but we couldn't find anything to photograph. But once we had the Brendan attachment, it made sense to make a work in relation to the other pictures that Thomas was making.

TJC
I made a few pictures on Bute. There was a saint called Blane, which interested me. But more importantly I took my daughter Sophie for a drive to the northmost point of the island, and the road ends and Sophie said, 'Look dad at all these beautiful trees', which I hadn't noticed of course, and it was one of the ancient oak forests on Bute. I made my second saints picture there, called *A Quality of Dancing*, in honour of Brendan and Blane but also Sophie for telling me to stop, slow down, open my eyes and pay attention.

Then a few years later, in 2013, I was given an opportunity to make work in Ireland. I had this thought that okay, Columba was born in County Donegal and then travelled with some difficulty across the country. But nobody knew how he did it. Kate suggested that our daughter Laura could help me; we travelled to Belfast and headed directly to the wilds of Donegal to find Columba's birth site at Gartan. I've tried physically and mentally, conceptually, to reconstruct how this young, very powerful rich kid ends up being able to get across from the far north and west of Ireland to the eastmost point of Ireland, called Burr Point.

Just south of Burr Point is Downpatrick. Laura and I finished making this picture at the Quoile River, burial site of Saints Patrick, Columba and Bride. We raced to get the ferry. We had to race – it was late, of course … I never pay attention to time. And we were just hurtling down the road. A big rainstorm had occurred, and it finally abated and all of a sudden, at the end of the daylight, this extraordinary serial group of rainbows started to appear one after another as if we were driving into them. Five or six occurred and then ten, twelve, twenty, thirty, forty. Surely over a hundred, maybe even hundreds. Laura and I were just astonished. They never stopped on either side, in front, rainbows everywhere. I've never seen anything like it. They just made us both laugh and feel quite wonderful. And it seemed to suggest that maybe something really special actually both had happened and was going to continue to happen with the Saints project.

AL
What initially drew you to the Celtic saints as a project?

CM
Their proximity, because they were local, but also incredible arrogance on my part because I thought there could only be six at the most, no more than that. There's over 600. We did an exhibition at Glasgow Cathedral and Govan Old Parish in 2015 – by then we were already aware that there were a lot more, but it was too daunting to really tackle. So we just started doing the odd day trip.

I like them because no one really knows anything about them. We know they existed. We don't know what they had for breakfast. I like that. In the age where we know so much, I think it's just a tremendously freeing opportunity to do what you like, write a new story.

TJC
But also the telling of the saintly stories, the narrative is, in my opinion, more or less both essential and elemental to the project we're on; the kinds of things that I'm interested in, in general. How does one, how does anyone tell a story? What kinds of stories are considered interesting and/ or important enough to be remembered? And I'm really interested in that;

Kate taught me a little bit more about the stories. In telling me, she was guiding my thought process of how to prepare myself to become acquainted with a saint's site once I reached it.

I was filled with these stories and the effect was exuberance, and it just did something to me like I've almost hardly ever experienced. This happened over and over, and then Kate would leave me for several hours to become acquainted enough with the place to work the site. And then when she could, she would join me and look through the camera to see if what I thought was good enough for her. If it was in those moments, I made the picture; if it wasn't, I said, 'Okay, fine, I'll make something else.'

Here is somebody who knows enough about not only the place, but the way I think about making pictures that can guide me, and I just thought, I'm having fun. This is great. I'm making better pictures – looser, by which I mean less constructively tight pictures than I've made in perhaps years.

AL
It sounds like the partnership worked well?

TJC
It was wonderful.

CM
We don't usually work together, we usually work separately. This project allowed us to work from home. I thought it'd be something that we could do together that would go on for a very long time, as a sort of way of doing something together that Thomas enjoyed.

It was completely devolved power. Thomas makes the pictures, I do the research and the driving; Thomas prints the pictures, we look at them together and then decide if we're going to use them or not, but we don't tread on each other's toes.

AL
How did the project evolve?

TJC
Out of the blue I was asked by a woman named Kamni Gill of the *Journal of Landscape Architecture* if I wanted to produce work for their visual section called 'Thinking Eye'. I told her about the Saints project in progress and she published ten to twelve pictures which were called 'Wandering Home: Following the Celtic Peregrinati'. It suggested to me that this was a real project.

And that's when I started to become aware that maybe I had assumed the authorship of something that didn't really belong to me; that I just jumped in (often enough as males of a certain age always seem to do) and assumed that something I was told about, that was originated by somebody else and where I was guided through to finding elements of the greatest joy both in the act of making and the actual picturing events themselves, I automatically seemed to think, I seemed to believe that all this was something that I was the author of. After this publication it became really clear to me that it wasn't the case. And that actually Kate had originated a project that I was the collaborating 'illuminator' of, as I've styled myself now.

I found from that point on that I did not have the responsibilities of actual authorship, I just had the pure, complete spontaneous personal joy of picture making, without any hassles at all, for one of the very first times in my long working life, and it just was thrilling, it was a relief and a release – and it became the greatest of joys.

AL
From the original title, 'Wandering Home', you have now settled on the title 'Desire Lines' – can you say more about its meaning?

CM
'Wandering Home' was a reference to our journeys to and from Glasgow and home in pursuit of making pictures. I think there are two meanings to 'Desire Lines'. One is a term used by town planners to describe the route when people don't follow the path, they just take the shortest line between two points. That's what a desire line is. If you think about the Celtic saints living out their lives, making a desire line to their own personal goal, but also through territory, that's how I see desire lines – both real and imaginary. Incidentally, 'Desire Lines' became a personal atlas of our home, a redrawing of the interior of our Caledonia.

AL
The book is laid out as a Calendar of Saints, a long-standing tradition of organising the Christian church year by liturgical seasons and arranging the

order of saints according to their feast days. Why did you structure the book this way?

CM
I used to work in Special Collections at Glasgow University. They have these books of hours; tiny vellum books that are highly illuminated which would be given as gifts and pass through a family. They were clearly people's personal objects. Every monastery, every house would have its own Calendar of Saints. They would all be the same in that they would include Jesus and the Holy Family and probably a national saint like St Andrew (who died in the year 60), but that would only be for maybe twenty days of the year, and that leaves you the rest of the year to fill up with your favourites. So we're saying that this Caledonian calendar could be your own personal object. There'll be some pages that aren't full because there's a blank page, which means you could stick your own picture in, you could write in it, you could put down people's birthdays opposite if you wanted to.

I would see the book as something that you would change, turn the page occasionally. I see the book as being something that you would have left open rather than closed on your coffee table. That's how I saw it. It's a much more spatial time-based object than a book that one would consume from cover to cover to finish it.

AL
How did you decide which saints to include in the project? And how difficult was it to locate female saints?

CM
Saints were good people that didn't have to pass a test approved by a bunch of bishops. And in fact, only two or three of these saints – Columba, Bride, Patrick – are recognised by the Roman church, but the rest are not. It might be a saint is a person knowledgeable about homoeopathy or palliative care, or education or guidance in navigation. These people didn't have supernatural powers, but they were recognised as special in their own lifetime and we remember when they died, on their feast day. Some of the saints were included because they were born in a month where there weren't so many people who died. Some months were very cluttered, we had to find a balance.

At the time, many centuries ago, people remembered and reported that there were as many female saints as there were male saints. I originally thought that maybe the book should only have as many female saints as male saints, but that would leave us with only forty pictures. In the end, I tried to have as many female saints as I could find, which was hard. Not only are they hard to find out about, but the places that they resided in or are associated with are difficult to get to. And they're often quite hidden places.

One of the things that became apparent as we visited places is that people had a personality and that most of the females were in hiding. Whereas Columba is on a cliff face, standing probably naked into the wind stopping everything.

In the case of St Enoch, rather than building a church and preserving it, they just completely expunged her and put an underground railway in the middle of the site. In the case of St Findoc, who lived on Loch Awe, no one is entirely sure who she was.

AL
Who is the earliest saint to feature in the project?

TJC
That's St Ninian, the first saint in Scotland. He made the first consecrated church in the country at Whithorn in the fifth century. He died in 432.

CM
We went to Whithorn in Dumfries and Galloway, and I did what I normally do, which is I drive and tell Thomas the story, and then he goes away for hours, and I just wait for him and have a sleep. Anyway, when I turned the car around, to have a nice view while I waited, the sat nav changed location as well to show what was in front. It showed a map with Ireland to the north of Wales, all these places that all our people were going to and from, and suddenly you realise that although it's taken us five and a half hours to get to it, what feels like the end of the world is actually in the middle of this tremendous ferment and it's not at all remote, it is actually really close. The Celtic travellers would have travelled by sea and by following rivers, and we go by stupid roads and walking. The Celtic people would have travelled along roads left behind by the Roman occupation. If you adjust your point of view, you suddenly see the world

has been completely accessible. If we could have sailed, it would have been so much easier to do this process.

AL
Given the peripatetic nature of these people, who were travelling by boat, by foot, when you had this sat-nav epiphany, did that then change how you were approaching the project in terms of determining where you would photograph or set up?

CM
It made me more determined to go to more remote places. What I did was I made a biography for every saint that I could find out about, because all the information comes from different places. And then I made pages for each location – map printouts – and then I made a little piece of information or story for Thomas for each place. And I worked out what boat we have to get, how many hours it's going to take. And I looked for places to visit, and even if they were a very long way away, I'd maybe try and go to six other places in one day to cover as much ground as possible.

In doing that, what I realised was that we actually covered the same territory St Mungo would have done endlessly, because we're making the same journey to and from Glasgow. We ended up doing the same kind of peripatetic journeys that the Celtic traveller would have made on foot over months.

TJC
What is interesting in relation to that is that there are about 600 historically recorded Celtic saints, and there are at least 5,000 historically recorded sites. But to my knowledge, most of the people that write about the saints don't go into the field and try and relocate and discover what the sites might look and feel like. And of the 5,000, Kate and I literally went to 1,250. I made 350 pictures, which we narrowed down to 125, and 79 of them are in this Calendar of Saints.

We made a cut-off point to restrict the number of saints that we could include as being about AD 850. Because in 850 there was a plague and famine, and we have the Viking raids that started, at which point you've got the Viking influence and Christianity changes again; Lindisfarne is destroyed by 850.

AL
Do you have a favourite saint?

TJC
I have two or three favourite saints, but St Fillan is the first, and St Kessog the original patron saint of Scotland is probably second, and then maybe Cuthbert is third. But I like Fillan because first the sites we found for him were always water based and quite exceptional. As places they were of personal allure to me, but the fact of his saintly patronage for the mentally ill and his personal work with the afflicted, to help if not cure them, to at least stabilise them, just warmed him narratively to my heart. And I found those sites particularly intimate and peculiarly compelling so I just by accident found that wow! What a place he liked to work in! What a guy! And the pictures, I think, reflect the kind of peculiar sense of affection. But the stories that accrue from him, in the sites that we found in a way dedicated to his followers and their pilgrimages towards him, just charm me in every possible way. Something about this person must have been genuinely wonderful. I was knocked out, and hope some of our St Fillan pictures convey some of this.

CM
I think St Medan must have been pretty tough; she supposedly educated St Enoch. She might be the person whom Edinburgh is named after. And if you go south of Edinburgh, to Nunraw and up towards Innerleithen, you see some of the places these people lived. Living there must have been hard. I thought the personality of Cuthbert was very joyful, very lush. Can you have favourites? Yes of course you can have favourites! I like St Kessog a lot. Also, I liked the fact that his name is spelled differently. Sometimes it ends with a G, sometimes there's CK, and I like all these ambiguities. I'm lucky we don't have any sons because I probably would have named them Kessog at this point.

AL
The photographs seemingly present the viewer with scenes of undisturbed nature – almost as though transporting the viewer back through time. How conscious were you of evoking this feeling of timelessness? And did this have a bearing on deciding the exact location of the photographs?

TJC
We went through so many sites, and began to find similarities; most of the sites had three obvious things in common. They were all easily accessible and exitable and of course, all of these sites have supplies of fresh water. Now, that seemed also necessarily obvious because if you bring groups of people together, they need to refresh themselves. And I'm presuming that it was also incredibly useful because at some point baptisms were going to occur and the fresh water that was so pure in those times was easily sanctifiable into the holy water for baptism. But then Kate found something that just absolutely gobsmacked me.

CM
Without exception all the sites have food on them: sorrel, spinach, rhubarb, berries, nuts, it's all there. There's no reason why you couldn't have been at any of these places for some time, they're all habitable.

TJC
And so, once it became clear that there were these three definitive elements available, then approaching the sites out of the blue became more coherent. Whatever the time is between then and now, more than a thousand years, sites don't change. Geographical sites will change of course because water sites do vary, but the conditions of the sites will remain relatively similar unless they're industrialised or urbanised.

CM
That's important to say. The reason I thought this would be an exciting project was when we first went to Culross I realised the landscape hadn't changed since the time of St Mungo and therefore we would be able to see Scotland's topography hadn't changed that much. I mean, outside of urbanisation.

AL
I think it's interesting that you had this feel for when you were in a spiritual place, when it would appear to make sense to you, but was there ever any doubt in your mind that you were at the right place?

CM
We believed everything that was written about the Celtic saints, but when we went to some places, it just didn't feel right. Watercourses had changed. And then there were other places we went to like Galloway, where the mono cattle culture is so strong. There's nothing left – it's just naked. Agricultural business has destroyed anything natural so there was little to see. The same goes when there's been intense forestry activity, where they've just ploughed everything up, but it takes away what was there.

TJC
Doubt is really a good word, especially when a person's name is Thomas. For me the sense of authenticity of the site began to be either clearly available or obviously artificial. At some point, some sites marked as historical just are either improbable or inauthentic.

CM
One site stands out: Holystone. It's near Otterburn in Northumberland. It's a baptism pool. And it's just very high up and although it's been preserved – some Victorians put a pool in with a cross and they cut grass and they put cordons around – if you look around it is an absolutely fantastic location, as high up as I've ever been in Britain. And you can see in every direction from there, and there's a thunderstruck tree.
    I got to a point where I didn't leave the car but Thomas came back in tears and said you've got to come and see this.

TJC
The pool is ringed by trees and the trees are old. There's something about the nature of the site. It's more or less on a sloping edge of a field. And then at the top of the slope the view is almost from the hills to the far coast. It's exceptionally, shiveringly authentic.

AL
What was the most challenging location to reach?

CM
Most places were reasonably okay to get to. What was really challenging was how much pollution there is, wherever you go, when you start to look. Thomas checks there are no wires. We have to feel there's no vibration (for the exposure). That there's no traffic. And then you realise there's a fence

post, you realise there are reflections from cars going past. The stuff we leave behind endures. It goes on and on, it's not just bits of glass or cigarette butts; when you go to the islands on Loch Lomond people just leave their entire sets of clothes and a tent behind. We went to one place and we remarked how clean it was, and then we met some people who were picking up litter, and they do it *every day*. We talk about a climate emergency, but it's much closer than that. It's what have you done with your takeaway? Or your bottle of water you couldn't live without? It's disgusting.

TJC
I realised that doing this, it's not 'artificialising' contemporary landscape into some romantic idea of previous time. It's simply reminding ourselves that the natural world doesn't have refuse and the leaves decompose, animal droppings disappear into the land, bodies do the same thing. There's nothing that doesn't re-enter the system that is naturally made. What we do by removing the detritus is to remind us of what is normal. It's not making something pretty or attempting to make something pretty. It's just simply trying to make something normal again.

AL
How far is the geographical spread of the project?

CM
Originally I thought that it would be across the Celtic world, so it would go over to Hibernia/Ireland, down to Wales, through Cornwall, to the top of France – Brittany. However, the Covid-19 pandemic presented us with a wonderful opportunity to work intensively from home. And that's what we did. We only worked as far as you could drive in one day.

When I was looking for information about the project, I was repeatedly frustrated that there were no Scottish maps really until Joan Blaeu's atlas, which is from the 1600s. However, I could not believe there weren't any maps. The Romans circumnavigated Britain in about AD 97. Ptolemy's map of Britain and Caledonia was made in about AD 150. I eventually asked a friend who knew about these things, and they said that there *were* maps. People always had maps, but they were more like shopping lists. They would be bespoke – if you asked me how to go somewhere, I would draw it for you. But they were personal things, they weren't mass-produced Ordnance Survey maps and they weren't things that people kept. People just used them, as a personal geography. There were no official maps compared to what we have now.

AL
The themes of wandering and faith are strong throughout the book – does that resonate for each of you? And do either of you consider yourself to be spiritual?

CM
Up until the pandemic, I was a regular churchgoer, and I'm a member of the Religious Society of Friends. However, since then, I have not been back, and I have no interest in going back to organised religion, and I have only been interested in being outdoors. The pandemic was an opportunity for pause and a reset and I realised that I'm not particularly interested in architecture. I don't see the need for it any more.

TJC
I will specifically suggest that I think Kate is, in my experience, one of the most spiritually realised people that I've ever met. Now, I'm not a spiritual person, I yearn for it, but I am not capable of it. I've never said this to anybody before, but part of the joy I've received in the Saints project is that something came back to me, whilst working with Kate, through Kate and because of Kate and for Kate.

Kate's saints work allowed me to return to everything that was basic and true and valuable in my work: intimacy, lyricism, ordinariness of places that surround all of us, in passing and without notice. When Kate says she'd rather be outside, that's exactly where I am with her. Because she's taught me again what I grew up knowing but managed to forget as an adult: this instinctual sense that we belong anywhere we find ourselves, if we're able to become familiar with it. Making pictures within places allows me the opportunity to become at least momentarily familiar with them. To attempt to recognise a place's uniqueness, and to respectfully attend to it with pictures, is my greatest joy.

AL
There's a genuine interest and curiosity about the devotion of these early

saints and the people that followed them. But then there's the devotion that you each have to the project, which sounds to me almost like a blind faith.

TJC
Actually, it's a redemptive faith. One of the several reasons why I am not able to be spiritual is that I'm too critical. I don't have an opened consciousness. It's too alert, and I'm a Thomas on purpose, I don't believe anything I can't touch or see. But I've trained myself to both see and touch deeply into areas where most people pass over. So devotion is absolutely the right phrase, and in certain devotional circles, the phrase goes 'love, devotion, surrender'.

AL
While the work you have produced over the last six decades has engaged with the landscape consistently, conceptually it seems that the Saints project is a return to your early practice and more aligned with Richard Long and Hamish Fulton than ever before – would you agree?

TJC
Uncategorically. I came here to Britain, partially in the first case because, especially in the early Seventies, both Long and Fulton – but particularly, then, Hamish and his work – had a lyrical quality to it that I had never experienced seeing before, except separately in either poetry or in paintings. They were wonderful works and they remain wonderful works and important works. But to be honest with you, it's the lyricism: How do you make something personal again, out of the 'bypass-able'? They were really masters at it and I intuitively started out in that manner. And I thought I could approach the lyrical through the extreme slowness of working with a nineteenth-century camera in the mid-twentieth century / early twenty-first century.

   The Saints pictures immediately reminded me of early works that I made in California and in New Mexico, where the opportunity to make pictures was singular and not the plural of projects that I have abandoned myself joyfully into now. I always knew that if I stood somewhere long enough a picture would call me. I always knew this. My first ten years of picture making were about waiting for the picture, the place, to call me. The picture and the place always called. I relearnt these early lessons, refreshed and anew, with Kate's Saints project – and because of her, have made some of the most beautiful and original, small lyrical pictures I have ever made.

AL
The physical prints for the Saints project are 8 by 10 inches, considerably smaller than your past work. Can you tell us more about this decision to print at this size?

TJC
I set out to make the most beautiful and diverse group of small pictures on a physical level that I've ever made in my life, to test the limits of my fifty-plus years of printing skills. I tried to do certain things, having made types of pictures that did various things within the context of the lyrical and of the immediate and of the intimate. Those three, structural, discipline areas of approach then allowed me to try and decide if and how to make a group of pictures that are essentially of 'bushes' interesting.

   And maybe I can't, but I thought okay, I *can*, because I'm interested in how even 'bushes' may be seen as unique. That is finally then how I began to approach the printing. Each picture is unique. All my pictures look more or less like all the others. But the printing process that I use now – and have for years, but specifically developed to the zenith that I have never achieved previously – is to make this group of what I call unique variants.

   The prints are each remarkably individualistic. The printed pictures are approached, as I do always, as objects to be considered both visually and tactilely. This was the other thing. I wanted the tonal conditions rendered within the very small, compact surfaces of the 8 by 10 to be as physically acute as possible, so they felt touchable, whereas a lot of photographs are essentially visual, as surface objects without touch – they're flat. I wanted my printed pictures to have the illusion of tactile depth, with as much tonal separation as was possible to make. There are very few people in the world that can do this. It just made me happy because that way the invisible became visible, and that is the essence of all my pictures. They should be felt but not recognisably seen.

AL
That's the perfect metaphor for this project; the saints are felt but not seen.

DESIRE LINES: A YEAR OF CELTIC SAINTS

JANUARY | page 18

7 January St Kentigerna
9 January St Fillan
13 January St Mungo
21 January St Winnin
29 January St Gildas
31 January St M'Aedóc

FEBRUARY | page 30

1 February St Bride
9 February St Ronan
9 February St Teilo

MARCH | page 35

6 March St Baldred
10 March St Kessog
11 March St Constantine
13 March St Quivox
13 March St Kennera
16 March St Boniface
17 March St Patrick
20 March St Cuthbert

APRIL | page 48

17 April St Donnan
18 April St Molaise

MAY | page 51

1 May St Asaph
16 May St Brendan
25 May St Bede
25 May St Dúnchad

JUNE | page 56

9 June St Columba
9 June St Báithíne
25 June St Moluag

JULY | page 60

1 July St Serf
6 July St Palladius
7 July St Boisil
18 July St Enoch

AUGUST | page 65

4 August St Berchán
5 August St Oswald
10 August St Blane
11 August St Angus
20 August St Oswine
23 August St Ebba
27 August St Maelruba
31 August St Aidan

SEPTEMBER | page 75

15 September St Mirren
16 September St Ninian
23 September St Adomnán
25 September St Cadoc
28 September St Conval

OCTOBER | page 80

8 October St Triduana
11 October St Kenneth
13 October St Findoc
21 October St Mun
25 October St Ernán
31 October St Begha

NOVEMBER | page 90

1 November St Maura
3 November St Baya
11 November St Martin
12 November St Machar
13 November St Devenick
15 November St Malo
17 November St Hilda
19 November St Medan

DECEMBER | page 101

2 December St Ethernan
23 December St Caran
23 December St Fittick

UNKNOWN | page 104

St Aibind
St Marion

ST KENTIGERNA Preaching place, Port Bawn, Inchcailloch, Loch Lomond, Stirling, Scotland, 2018

ST FILLAN Healing Pool, Loch Earn at the River Earn, St Fillans, Breadalbane, Perth and Kinross, Scotland, 2018

ST FILLAN *Vespers* – preaching place, Loch Earn, St Fillans, Breadalbane, Perth and Kinross, Scotland, 2018

ST FILLAN Death site, reflections, River Lochay, Killin, Breadalbane, Stirling, Scotland, 2018

ST MUNGO St Mungo's Well, Ruthven Water, Perth and Kinross, Scotland, 2018

ST MUNGO Perceiving Burn, Tundergarth, Dumfries and Galloway, Scotland, 2020

ST MUNGO Looking into the sun – *None*, Cranshaws, Scottish Borders, Scotland, 2019

ST WINNIN Possibly buried here, Abbey grounds, River Garnock, Sagtoun, Kilwinning, North Ayrshire, Scotland, 2018

ST GILDAS Born on the banks of the Firth of Clyde, Skelmorlie, North Ayrshire, Scotland, 2018

ST M'AEDÓC Pow of Errol, Port Allen, Perth and Kinross, Scotland, 2020

ST M'AEDÓC Summer whiteout – chamomile field, Port Allen, Perth and Kinross, Scotland, 2020

ST BRIDE Harleyholm, South Lanarkshire, Scotland, 2020

ST BRIDE River Wampool, Whitrigg, Cumberland, England, 2020

ST RONAN North Sea, Berwick-upon-Tweed, Northumberland, England, 2020

ST TEILO Next to his dedicated well, Mouse Water, Cleghorn, South Lanarkshire, Scotland, 2020

ST BALDRED Next to St Baldred's Cave and Bed, St Baldred's Garden, Seacliff, North Sea, East Lothian, Scotland, 2019

ST KESSOG Inchtavannach, Loch Lomond, Argyll and Bute, Scotland, 2015

ST KESSOG Martyred at Bandry Bay, Loch Lomond, Argyll and Bute, Scotland, 2015

ST CONSTANTINE Death site, *Vespers*, Machrihanish, Mull of Kintyre, Argyll and Bute, Scotland, 2019

ST QUIVOX River Ayr, South Ayrshire, Scotland, 2019

ST KENNERA Crab apple and hawthorn blossom, Kirkinner, Dumfries and Galloway, Scotland, 2019

ST BONIFACE Bright afternoon light, Chanonry Point, Rosemarkie Bay, Moray Firth, Highland, Scotland, 2019

ST PATRICK High tide – *Terce*, looking back towards Hibernia, Port of Spittal Bay, Dumfries and Galloway, Scotland, 2019

ST PATRICK Burial site along with St Columba and St Brigit, River Quoile, Downpatrick, County Down, Northern Ireland, 2013

ST CUTHBERT Cuddy's Well, Bellingham, River North Tyne, Northumberland, England, 2020

ST DONNAN *Vespers*, Kildonan, Isle of Arran, Firth of Clyde, North Ayrshire, Scotland, 2019

ST DONNAN St Donnan's Seat, Helmsdale, Highland, Scotland, 2020

ST MOLAISE Refuge and restoration, St Molaise's Cave, Holy Isle, Lamlash Bay, North Ayrshire, Scotland, 2019

ST ASAPH Death site, black poplars along the River Elwy, St Asaph, Denbighshire, Wales, 2020

ST BRENDAN Looking towards Ultima Thule, Sango Bay, Durness, Highland, Scotland, 2013

ST BEDE Monkwearmouth, Sunderland, Tyne and Wear, England, 2020

ST DÚNCHAD Kilconquhar Loch, Kilconquhar, Fife, Scotland, 2015

ST COLMÁN Summer solstice, *Sext*, Lake of Menteith, Inchmahome, Stirling, Scotland, 2019

ST COLUMBA Hinba reclaimed, Easdale, Firth of Lorn, Argyll and Bute, Scotland, 2019

ST BÁITHÍNE *Evensong*, Abbey St Bathans, Scottish Borders, Scotland, 2019

ST MOLUAG Rosemarkie, Black Isle, Highland, Scotland, 2019

ST SERF Woodhill, Alva, Clackmannanshire, Scotland, 2018

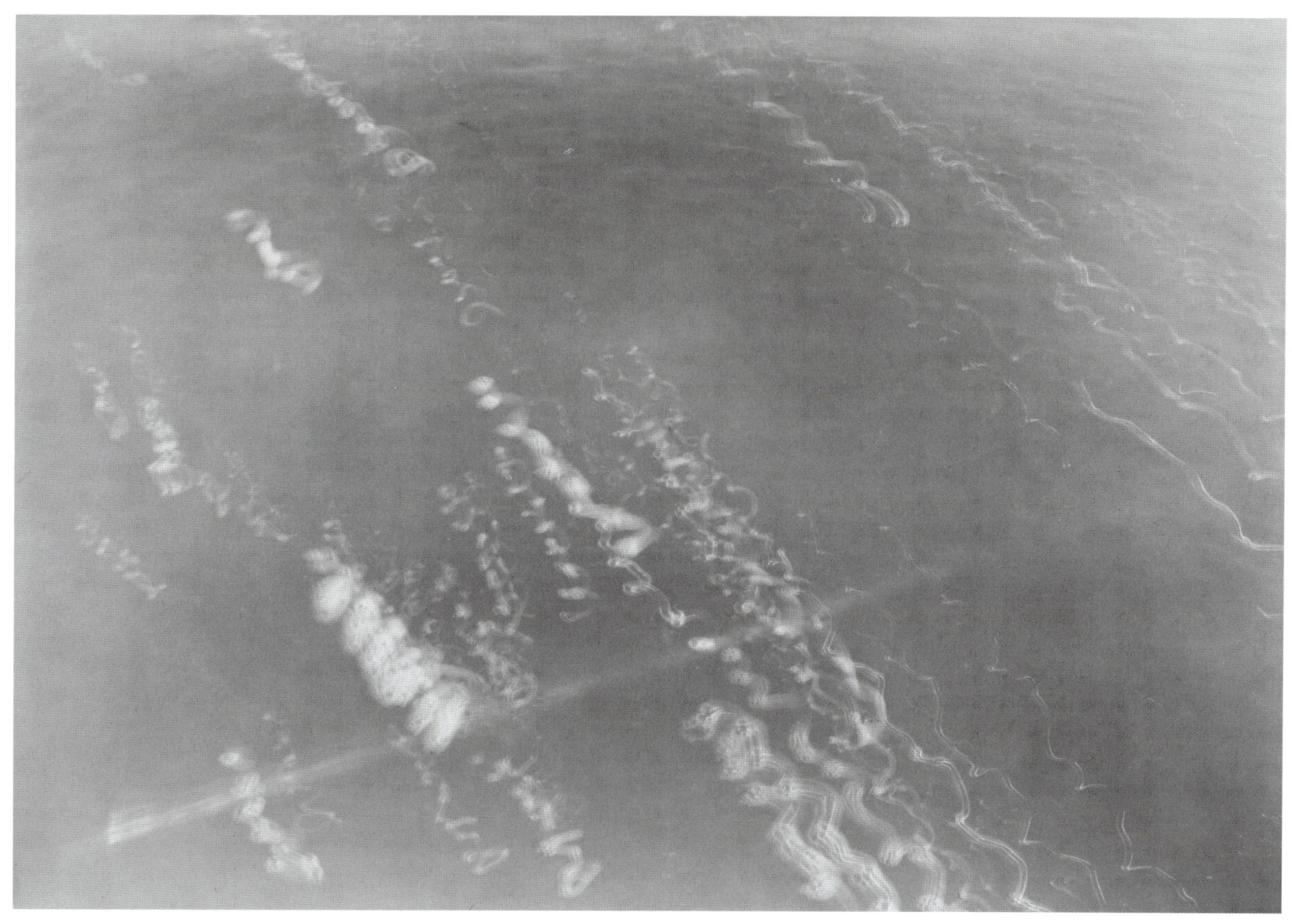

ST SERF Flightpath – an indication of the arrival of St Enoch and St Mungo, Firth of Forth, Culross, Fife, Scotland, 2015

ST PALLADIUS Paldyfair Wood, Auchenblae, Aberdeenshire, Scotland, 2020

ST BOISIL Ancient apple orchard, Melrose, Scottish Borders, Scotland, 2019

ST ENOCH Where she was set adrift, Aberlady, East Lothian, Scotland, 2015

ST BERCHÁN Failing light, *Vespers*, Burntshields, Kilbarchan, Renfrewshire, Scotland, 2018

ST OSWALD Raven Beck, Kirkoswald, Westmorland and Furness, England, 2020

ST BLANE A Quality of Dancing, ancient oak forest near Balnakailly Burn, Isle of Bute, Argyll and Bute, Scotland, 2002

ST ANGUS Withdrawing summer evening, *Compline*, Loch Voil, Stirling, Scotland, 2019

ST OSWINE Death site where he was martyred, Gilling West, North Yorkshire, England, 2020

ST EBBA Windblown leaves and rowan berries, Ebchester, County Durham, England, 2020

ST MAELRUBA Looking towards Raasay, Applecross Bay, Applecross, Wester Ross, Highland, Scotland, 2020

ST AIDAN Windblown hawthorn blossoms and daisy field, River Tweed, Melrose, Scottish Borders, Scotland, 2015

ST AIDAN Moray Firth, Burghead, Moray, Scotland, 2018

ST MIRREN Next to his preferred route when travelling north, Colzium Burn, Colzium, North Lanarkshire, Scotland, 2020

ST NINIAN Lady's Well, Holystone, Northumberland, England, 2020

ST ADOMNÁN Thornton Burn, Innerwick, East Lothian, Scotland, 2019

ST CADOC Cathkin Braes, South Lanarkshire, Scotland, 2019

ST CONVAL Glaisnock Water, Cumnock, East Ayrshire, Scotland, 2018

ST TRIDUANA Retreat, Roscobie, Fife, Scotland, 2020

ST TRIDUANA Death site, Restalrig, Edinburgh, Scotland, 2018

ST KENNETH River Eden, Clutes Mill, Fife, Scotland, 2018

ST FINDOC Loch Awe, Argyll and Bute, 2019

ST MUN River Eachaig, Holy Loch, Argyll and Bute, Scotland, 2018

ST ERNÁN *Terce*, Assloss Water, Kilmarnock, East Ayrshire, Scotland, 2020

ST BEGHA Dunbar, East Lothian, Scotland, 2019

ST BEGHA Dunbar, East Lothian, Scotland, 2020

ST MAURA Wild shimmering hawthorn blossom, Annick Water, Dreghorn, North Ayrshire, 2019

ST BAYA Summer apples, Cathedral of The Isles, Millport, Cumbrae, North Ayrshire, Scotland, 2018

ST MARTIN Mist and daisies, Kilmartin, Argyll and Bute, Scotland, 2020

ST MACHAR *None*, River Don, Aberdeen, Aberdeenshire, Scotland, 2020

ST DEVENICK *Vespers*, Causey Mounth, Banchory, Aberdeenshire, Scotland, 2020

ST MALO River Nethan, South Lanarkshire, Scotland, 2020

ST HILDA Windy evening, North Sea, Whitby Abbey, North Yorkshire, England, 2020

ST HILDA Evening sunburst, the death site where St Begu witnessed St Hilda's soul being borne to heaven by angels, Hackness, North Yorkshire, England, 2020

ST MEDAN Cailiness Point, Luce Bay, Solway Firth, Dumfries and Galloway, Scotland, 2019

ST MODWENNA Huntly Burn, Longforgan, Perth and Kinross, Scotland, 2020

ST EIDYN *Vigil*, looking north towards Traprain Law, Berwick Law and Bass Rock from White Castle, Nunraw, East Lothian, Scotland, 2019

ST ETHERNAN Pilgrim Bay, Isle of May, Firth of Forth, Fife, Scotland, 2018

ST CARAN St Kieran's Well, Cowie Water, Fetteresso, Aberdeenshire, Scotland, 2020

ST FITTICK Site where he was washed up after being thrown from a ship and went on to establish a church, Nigg, Easter Ross, Highland, Scotland, 2019

ST AIBIND Only remembered here, Cawdor, Highland, Scotland, 2019

ST MARION Believed to be the daughter of a local family, Glen Strathfarrar, Kilmorack, Sutherland, Scotland, 2019

BIOGRAPHIES OF THE SAINTS

Shrouded in the mists of time, myth, legend and story, much supposed information about the saints can never be entirely correct or possible. We invite you to think of the following biographies as sketches made in good faith. The saints featured in this list are thought to have been active in the locations featured in this book.

A saint in the Middle Ages was a good person, recognised within their lifetime. But a saint was not destined to be remembered unless they had a feast day: a specific date when their life has been marked through the ensuing centuries. In times when travel and communication were much more difficult than today, each place evolved to have its own calendar of feast days. And so, even the dates associated with each saint are not concrete.

In this book, we have used the most consistent approach that we can, where there are choices, by opting for the dates that are believed to be the anniversary of the death of the saint, using sources such as the sixteenth-century *Aberdeen Breviary* and the 'Commemorations of Saints in Scottish Place-Names' project undertaken by the University of Glasgow's School of Humanities since 2010. While the death site and date are the most reliable information available, the place and date of birth are often either unclear or not recorded, and so this information is omitted in some cases below. Another element of confusion is the duplication of names: the same name has sometimes been shared by several different people whose identities are thought to have merged through time under one saint's name.

ST ADOMNÁN
(b. 627, Argyll; d. 23 September 704). Feast day 23 September. Ninth Abbot of Iona in 679. Biographer of St Columba, and historian of the early Celtic church.

ST AIBIND OF MANE / Éibhinn / Aoibhinn
Forgotten feast day. Very little is known about this female saint. She is only remembered at St Barevan's Church, Cawdor, Highland.

ST AIDAN
(b. 590, Ireland; d. 31 August 651, Bamburgh, Northumberland). Feast day 31 August. First bishop of Lindisfarne. He was well recorded by St Bede.

ST ANGUS
(b. 5th century, Ireland). Feast day 11 August. Associated with the village of Balquhidder.

ST ASAPH
(b. Britain; d. 1 May 596, St Asaph, Denbighshire). Feast day 1 May. Closely associated with St Mungo. Lived as a hermit, and founded a monastery in North Wales. The monastery and town are named after him.

ST BÁITHÍNE MAC BRÉNAIND
(b. Ireland; d. 600, Iona). Feast day 9 June. A disciple, companion and cousin of St Columba, and Prior of Hinba, the whereabouts of which is lost. Venerated in Ireland, especially Donegal, and at Abbey St Bathans, Scottish Borders.

ST BALDRED OF TYNINGHAME
(b. Northumberland; d. 6 March 757, Bass Rock, East Lothian). Feast day 6 March. Lived as a hermit opposite and on Bass Rock, and founded a monastery at Tyninghame. There are four churches devoted to him nearby.

ST BAYA
Feast day 3 November. Associated with Dunbar and with the Cumbrae Islands in the Firth of Clyde where there is a shrine dedicated to St Vey. Might be the same person as St Begha.

ST BEDE THE VENERABLE
(b. c.673, Jarrow, Northumberland; d. 25 May 735, Jarrow, Northumberland). Feast day 25 May. The greatest historian of the early church. Never left Northumberland but was fluent in Latin, Greek and Hebrew. He also wrote about natural history, poetry and scripture. Patron saint of English writers, historians and Jarrow.

ST BEGHA / Bee
(b. Ireland; d. 681, Northumberland). Feast day 31 October. Very little is known about her life. Reputed to have fled from Ireland to Cumberland, and to have founded a convent at Hartlepool – if indeed she existed.

ST BERCHÁN / Mobhí Cláraineach
(b. Glasnevin, Leinster; d. 12 October 544). Feast day 4 August in Scotland. Related to St Brigit of Kildare (St Bride). Poet and prophet. Patron of Kilbarchan.

ST BLANE / Bláán
(b. Bute; d. 590). Feast day 10 August. Active across the Central Belt of Scotland, most obviously associated with Dunblane. Patron saint of Kingarth, Bute and Dunblane.

ST BOISIL OF MELROSE
(b. Northumberland; d. 7 July 661, Melrose, Scottish Borders). Feast day 7 July. He was trained by St Aidan, became Prior of Melrose, and taught St Cuthbert at Melrose.

ST BONIFACE / Curetán
Feast day 16 March. Active in the 7th and 8th centuries at Cromarty Firth, Glen Glass, Loch Ness and Rosemarkie.

ST BRENDAN THE NAVIGATOR
(b. 484, Fenit Island, County Kerry; d. 577, Annaghdown, County Galway). Feast day 16 May. Patron saint of Cape Verde islands, mariners, travellers and whales. Fabled navigator who possibly sailed to America in a curragh. His voyages were immortalised in a book, *Navigatio Sancti Brendani Abbatis*. Remembered on St Kilda, South Uist, Mull, Seil, Islay and Kilbrannan Sound between Arran and Kintyre. Venerated on Bute where in 1355 the local men were known as the 'Brandanys off Bute'.

ST BRIGIT – *see* ST BRIDE

ST BRIDE / Brigit of Kildare
(b. 451, Dundalk, County Louth; d. 525, Kildare). Feast day 1 February. Popular saint remembered in many place names in Scotland. Patron saint of babies, blacksmiths, chicken farmers, healers, livestock and dairy workers, midwives, poets, the poor, unmarried parents and many more. Born a slave, she performed miracles from a young age. Recognised as special, she was freed. Went on to found a monastery at Kildare. It is not clear if she ever came to Scotland but her cult was prolific.

ST CADOC OF LLANCARFAN
(b. 497, Monmouthshire; d. 25 September 580). Feast day 25 September. Patron of famine victims, deafness and glandular disorders. Carmunnock is an ancient settlement associated with his missionary work.

ST CARAN / Cieran / Kieran
(5th century, Ireland). Feast day 23 December. Little is known about them or if they were a real person or a combination of people real and imagined.

ST COLMÁN – *see* **ST COLUMBA**

ST COLUMBA / Colmcille / Columb / Colmán / Commán / Mo Cholmóc / Mo Chommóc / Mo Chumma
(b. 7 December 521, Gartan, County Donegal; d. 9 June 597, Iona). Feast day 9 June. Patron saint of Derry, poets and bookbinders. Founded Iona Abbey in 563. Prolific missionary.

ST CONSTANTINE OF STRATHCLYDE
(b. 570; martyred 640, Machrihanish, Argyll and Bute defending Christians against Vikings). Feast day 11 March. He took the name Constantine after the Emperor; his given name is not known. His relics were kept in a shrine at Govan.

ST CONVAL OF INCHINNAN AND EASTWOOD
(b. 570, Ireland; d. 630). Feast day 28 September. Disciple of St Mungo and missionary. After a vision or dream he crossed the Irish Sea by surfing on a large stone and continued up the River Clyde to the River Cart. His 'Chariot' is preserved behind railings in the grounds of the Normandy Hotel, Renfrew.

ST CUTHBERT
(b. 634, Dunbar, Lothian; d. 20 March 687, Inner Farne, Northumberland). Feast day 20 March. Monk, bishop and in later life a hermit. Patron of Northumberland, which at that time would have included south-east Scotland.

ST DEVENICK
(d. 887, Caithness). Feast day 13 November. Possibly a disciple of St Columba. He is strongly associated with St Machar and the village of Banchory-Devenick, where there is an ancient droving road to Stonehaven and a fair named after him.

ST DONNAN THE GREAT / Donnán of Eigg
(b. 550, Ireland; martyred 17 April 617, Isle of Eigg). Feast day 17 April. A follower of St Columba. Active on the west coast of Scotland. Patron saint of Helmsdale and Isle of Eigg.

ST DÚNCHAD OF IONA / Dúnchad mac Cinn Fáelad
(b. Ireland; d. 717). Feast day 25 May. Eleventh Abbot of Iona.

ST EBBA OF COLDINGHAM
(b. 615, Northumberland; d. 23 August 683, Coldingham, Scottish Borders). Feast day 23 August. Sister of St Oswald. Founded monasteries at Ebchester and St Abb's Head.

ST EIDYN – *see* **ST MEDAN**

ST ENOCH / Tenew / Teneu / Thaney
(b. 510, Scotland; d. 570, Scotland). Feast day 18 July. Daughter of King Loth, taught by St Medan. Taken in by St Serf, she lived at Culross with her son, St Mungo. She followed her son to Glasgow, where her name is still remembered. Patron saint of unmarried mothers and Glasgow.

ST ERNÁN ABBOT OF HINBA / Marnan / Marnoch / Mo Ernin
(b. Ireland; d. 625, Iona). Feast day 25 October. Abbot of Hinba. Uncle of St Columba, and one of Columba's companions who travelled from Ireland to Iona. There are at least six people with the same name, venerated across Scotland. This St Ernán's relics were kept at Kilmarnock where he was the patron saint and namesake.

ST ETHERNAN
(Scottish martyr). Feast day 2 December. Possibly a monk on Iona.

ST FILLAN OF MUNSTER
(b. c.695, Ireland; d. 9 January 770). Feast day 9 January. Son of St Kentigerna. He laboured in the Strathfillan area. Patron saint of the mentally ill.

ST FINDOC OF INISHAIL
Feast day 13 October. Female saints believed to be local women associated with Inishail, Loch Awe, Argyll.

ST FITTICK / Fiacre / Photinus
(b. 600, Ireland; d. 670). Feast day 23 December. Possibly more than one person with the same name, maybe a Pictish person particular to Nigg, on the Moray Firth. Or he was educated in France, and in a storm washed ashore at Nigg Beach, where he found a well and built a church.

ST GILDAS THE WISE
(b. 500, Strathclyde; d. 29 January 570, Rhuys). Feast day 29 January. First historian of British history, author of *De Excidio et Conquestu Britanniae*.

ST HILDA OF WHITBY
(b. 614, Northumberland; d. 17 November 680, Hackness, North Yorkshire). Feast day 17 November. Founded an abbey at Whitby in 657 – a double monastery where men and women worshipped together but lived in separate houses. Insisted upon all property being held in common, and the virtues of peace and charity. In 664 she hosted the Synod of Whitby.

ST KENNERA – *see* ST QUIVOX
It is possible they were the same person.

ST KENNETH / Cainnech of Aghaboe / Canice
(b. 515, Dungiven, Derry-Londonderry; d. 599, Aghaboe, County Laois). Feast day 11 October. Abbot, priest, missionary. A contemporary of St Columba who visited Hinba. Dedicated churches on Kintyre, Mull, Iona, Coll, in Ayrshire and at Kilrymont, Fife.

ST KENTIGERNA
(b. Ireland; d. 734, Loch Lomond, Stirling). Feast day 7 January. Mother of St Fillan. They left Ireland as refugees. She settled as anchoress on Inchcailloch on Loch Lomond: the island is named after her, translated from Gaelic Innis na Cailleach, meaning 'Isle of the Old Woman'.

ST KESSOG / Macessog / Kessock
(b. 460, Cashel, Munster; martyred 10 March 520, Bandry Bay, Loch Lomond, Argyll and Bute). Feast day 10 March. Very active about Loch Lomond, Lennox and Perth and Kinross. Inspired a very large cult at Inchtavannach and was the patron saint of Scotland, until the relics of St Andrew the Apostle eclipsed his popularity.

ST MACHAR
(b. 540, Ireland; d. 600). Feast day 12 November. Patron saint of Aberdeen. Associated with St Columba, possibly one of his companions.

ST M'AEDÓC / Madoe / Aiden
(b. 550, County Cavan; d. 31 January 632, Ferns, County Wexford). Feast day 31 January. Remembered at St Madoes, and in the Carse of Gowrie area, Perth and Kinross.

ST MAELRUBA
(b. 3 January 642, Bangor, County Down; d. 21 April 722, Teampull, Highland). Feast day 27 August. He was active in Argyll and in 673 founded a monastery at Applecross.

ST MALO / Machutus
(b. 27 March 501, Gwent; d. 15 November 621, Saint-Malo, Brittany). Feast day 15 November. He was the favourite disciple of St Brendan the Navigator, who baptised him as an adult and whom he accompanied on some of his voyages. It is unlikely he ever lived in Scotland but there were several cults devoted to him there, such as at Lesmahagow.

ST MARION OF GLEN STRATHFARRAR
Forgotten feast day. A female saint. Remembered in the parish of Kilmorack, Highland. The suggestion is that she died young and was the daughter of a local noble family.

ST MARTIN OF TOURS
(b. 8 November 316, Hungary; d. 8 November 397, buried three days later, Tours). Feast day 11 November. A Roman soldier who became a monk and later an abbot. Very popular in the Middle Ages across Western Europe. He taught St Ninian, and was related to St Patrick. Patron saint of St Martin's Cathedral, Ypres, Belgium; Utrecht, Netherlands; and two towns in Poland.

ST MAURA
(d. Kilmaurs, East Ayrshire). Feast day 3 November. Possibly the sister of St Bride. She is associated with the Cumbrae Islands in the Firth of Clyde where she might have been instructed by St Baya. A church is dedicated to her on the Isle of Cumbrae.

ST MEDAN / Modwenna / Eidyn / Monenna / Medana / Maiden / Edana
(b. 435, Northern Ireland; d. c.517, Longforgan, Perth and Kinross). Feast day 19 November. Famed for her beautiful eyes. Ran away from a suitor to Rhins of Galloway, hid herself in a tree but was followed by the suitor. She then plucked out her eyes and threw them down; a spring of water appeared where the eyes landed, and she washed the blood from her face in the water. Similar to the myth of St Triduana. Founded seven churches in Scotland, including one where Edinburgh Castle stands. Edinburgh is named after her. Credited as being St Enoch's teacher. Patron saint of ophthalmologists.

ST MIRREN / Miren
(b. 565, Bangor, County Down; d. 620). Feast day 15 September. Irish monk, evangelist. Contemporary of St Columba. Founded a church at Seedhill on the banks of the White Cart Water. Patron saint of Paisley and its football team. His shrine in Paisley became a very important pilgrimage site.

ST MODWENNA – *see* **ST MEDAN**

ST MOLAISE / Mo Laise
(b. 566, Ireland; d. 639, Ireland). Feast day 18 April. Taught by St Mun. Lived as a hermit for several years on Holy Isle off the Isle of Arran in the Firth of Clyde. After visiting Rome he returned with the idea to adopt the Roman method of calculating Easter.

ST MOLUAG / Lughaidh
(b. Ireland; d. 592, Rosemarkie, Highland). Feast day 25 June. Worked amongst the Picts. He and his followers established a religious community on the Isle of Lismore in 562, plus ten churches and 100 monasteries. Patron saint of Argyll.

ST MUN / Munnu / Fintán of Taghmon
(b. Ireland; d. 21 October 635, Kilmun, Argyll and Bute). Feast day 21 October. Arrived in Scotland in 579. Two wolves helped him guard his sheep. Joined the monastery at Iona just after St Columba died. Went on to live as a hermit on an island on Loch Leven, and later founded a monastery at Kilmun.

ST MUNGO
(pet name meaning beloved) / Mo Cha / Kentigern
(b. 518, Culross, Fife; d. 13 January 612, Glasgow). Feast day 13 January. Patron saint of Glasgow, Penicuik and Scotland. Son of St Enoch. He lived until the age of 25 at St Serf's monastery at Culross. Missionary active throughout his life in the Central Belt of Scotland, Dumfries and Galloway and the Lake District. Founder of Glasgow.

ST NINIAN
(b. 360, Scotland; d. 432, Whithorn, Dumfries and Galloway). Feast day 16 September. Little is known about him or his identity; his name appears in many forms. One version of his identity suggests that he was probably British and studied in Rome. Sent by Pope Siricius to convert the Picts. He dedicated the first Christian church in Scotland to St Martin, in 397 at Whithorn.

ST OSWALD OF NORTHUMBERLAND
(b. 604, Deira; martyred 5 August 641, Maserfield, Oswestry, Shropshire). Feast day 5 August. Brother of St Ebba. Defender of the Christians, remembered at numerous places, especially battle sites.

ST OSWINE OF DEIRA
(d. 20 August 651, West Gilling, Yorkshire). Feast day 20 August. A devout Christian, raised in the Celtic tradition. Struggled to control his kingdom, and was murdered in an ambush.

ST PALLADIUS
(b. 5th century, in an unknown location outside Britain; d. Fordoun, Aberdeenshire). Feast day 6 July, known as Paldy Fair. Sent by Pope Celestine I to Scotland to challenge Pelagian heresy. Remembered near Fordoun at several places. Founded Paldy Kirk, where he preached and died.

ST PATRICK
(b. Britain; d. Ireland). Feast day 17 March. Celebrated across Scotland.

ST QUIVOX / Kevoc
(b. 4th century, Greece; martyr). Feast day 13 March. They might be male or female. The origin of the name St Quivox is very obscure. A village in South Ayrshire has the same name.

ST RONAN OF IONA
(b. 7th century, Ireland). Feast day 9 February. Not to be confused with the other eleven saints called Ronan. He is referred to by St Bede as having spoken at the Synod of Whitby in 660. Credited with driving the devil and paganism out of the Leithen Valley in the Scottish Borders.

ST SERF OF CULROSS / Serban / Servanus
(b. 500, Scotland; d. 583, Dunning, Perth and Kinross). Feast day 1 July. Founded a monastery at Culross. Active in Fife and Perth; many churches in the area named after him. He is closely associated with the life of St Kentigern, whom he named Mungo.

ST TEILO
(b. Penally, Pembrokeshire; d. 560, Llandeilo, Carmarthenshire). Feast day 9 February. Bishop of Llanduff and Llandeilo Fawr. Patron saint of fruit trees and horses.

ST TRIDUANA / Tredwell / Trodline / Trollhaene
(b. 320, possibly in Patras, Greece; d. 380, Restalrig, Edinburgh). Feast day 8 October. Accompanied St Regulus with the relics of St Andrew the Apostle to Scotland. A virgin who removed her eyes and sent them to a suitor: a similar story to St Medan and others.

ST WINNIN / Findbarr / Finnian
(b. 7th century; buried Kilwinning, North Ayrshire). Feast day 21 January. Arrived at the mouth of the River Garnock in 715. Actively converted the local people to Christianity and established places of worship. His miracle was that he changed the course of the River Garnock.

The Book © the Trustees of the National Galleries of Scotland, 2025
All pictures are © Thomas Joshua Cooper
Pictures selected by Catherine Mooney and Thomas Joshua Cooper
Picture sequence by Catherine Mooney

ISBN 978 1 911054 65 8

British Library Cataloguing-in-Publication Data
A catalogue record for this book is available from the British Library

Project Manager: Jonny Clowes
Copy-editor: Abigail Grater
Proofreader: Susan Milligan

Publishing Team
Publisher: Ann Crawford
Publishing Project Editor: Catherine Aitken
Publishing Co-ordinator: Jonny Clowes
Publishing Assistants: Hannah Killoh and Caitlin Mellon

Designed by Joe Ewart
Typeset in Appoline
Printed in tricolour on 170gsm Magno Matt Classic by Albe de Coker in Belgium

Front cover:
Thomas Joshua Cooper, *Perceiving Burn*, Tundergarth, Dumfries and Galloway, Scotland, 2020

All rights reserved. No part of this publication may be reproduced, stored in a retrieval system, or transmitted, in any form or by any means, without the prior permission in writing of the National Galleries of Scotland's Publishing Department, or as expressly permitted by law, by licence or under terms agreed with the appropriate reprographics rights organisation.

The proceeds from the sale of this book go towards supporting the National Galleries of Scotland. For a complete list of current publications, please write to: NGS Publishing at the National Galleries of Scotland, 70 Belford Road, Edinburgh EH4 3DE or visit our website: www.nationalgalleries.org

National Galleries of Scotland is a charity registered in Scotland (No. SC003728)

ACKNOWLEDGEMENTS

David Bellingham
Jenny Brownrigg
Laura Indigo Cooper
Frazer Capie
Revd Canon Robin Coutts
Professor Stephen Driscoll
Kamni Gill
Professor Vicky Gunn
Talitha Kotze
Sir John Leighton
Joe Logan
Anne Lyden
Professor Duncan Macmillan
Dr Kate Robinson